A LIFE
OF
LOVELY

Journal

PUBLISHING GROUP
Nashville, Tennessee

The quotes on these pages were taken from
*A Life of Lovely: The Young Woman's Guide
to Collecting the Moments That Matter*
by Annie F. Downs
B&H Publishing Group, 2019

978-1-5359-2378-1

Published by B&H Publishing Group
Nashville, Tennessee

Author represented by Alive Literary Agency,
7680 Goddard Street, Suite 200, Colorado Springs,
Colorado, 80920, www.aliveliterary.com.

1 2 3 4 5 6 7 8 • 23 22 21 20 19

WHEN YOU FIND JESUS, YOU HAVE FOUND LOVELY.

HE IS EVERYTHING WE NEED.

YOU ARE UNIQUE. YOU ARE THE ONLY YOU THERE IS.
GOD DID THAT ON PURPOSE.

THERE IS SOMETHING BEAUTIFUL, AND SOMETHING THAT OPENS
YOUR HEART IN NEW AND DEEPER WAYS, WHEN YOU OPEN
YOURSELF UP TO EXPERIENCE PAIN AS WELL AS JOY.

EVERY ACT OF OBEDIENCE IS AN ACT OF COURAGE.
EVERY HARD YES, EVERY DIFFICULT NO, EVERY MOMENT
OF MOVING AND SHAKING TAKES BRAVERY.

_____

_____

_____

_____

_____

_____

_____

_____

_____

_____

_____

_____

_____

_____

_____

_____

_____

_____

_____

_____

_____

GOD GIVES US PERMISSION TO FEEL.
WE DON'T HAVE TO NUMB THE PAIN.

THE ONLY WAY TO TRULY SEE BEAUTY, FOR MY HEART
TO GROW IN CAPACITY AND IN ABILITY TO LOVE AND CHERISH,
IS THROUGH PAIN AND HEARTACHE.

I SEE THE GOD WHO LIKES TO PUT THINGS BACK TOGETHER.
HE LOVES TO TAKE UGLY, MESSY THINGS (AND PEOPLE)
AND MAKE SENSE FROM THE CHAOS.

GOD IS ORDERING MY STEPS, GOD IS ORDERING ALL THINGS,
AND I REST IN THAT.

EVERY TEAR I'VE SOWN WILL GROW INTO SOMETHING JOYFUL
AND BEAUTIFUL, FAR GRANDER THAN I EVER EXPECTED.

THERE ARE PEOPLE WHO SEE YOU AND SEE YOUR LIFE
AND BECAUSE OF THE WAYS YOU REMIND THEM OF GOD,
THEY SEE HIM TOO.

MAYBE WHEN WE MAKE OUR HEARTS AVAILABLE TO THE
HARD MOMENTS AND ALLOW OURSELVES TO EXPERIENCE
GOD'S LOVE IN NEW WAYS, WE ARE ALSO INCREASING
OUR CAPACITY TO LOVE OTHERS.

I BELIEVE THAT HE IS WHO HOLDS ALL THINGS TOGETHER.

GOD WAS DOING A BIG WORK. I KNEW IT, I JUST HAD TO
KEEP SHOWING UP, EVEN WHEN IT HURT OR FELT HARD
OR WASN'T *AT ALL* WHAT I WANTED TO DO.

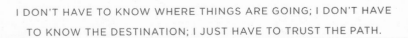

I DON'T HAVE TO KNOW WHERE THINGS ARE GOING; I DON'T HAVE
TO KNOW THE DESTINATION; I JUST HAVE TO TRUST THE PATH.

MAYBE THE MOST BEAUTIFUL THING WE CAN LOOK AT, IN ORDER
TO PERSEVERE, FINISH, THRIVE, LIVE, IS THE EYES OF OUR GOD.

KEEP LOOKING TO OUR GOD WHO HAS THE MASTER PLAN AND IS
WORKING ALL THINGS OUT FOR OUR GOOD EVEN WHEN WE'RE
ONLY SEEING A TINY CORNER OF HIS MASTERPIECE.

GRACE REMINDS ME LESS OF WHO I AM
AND MORE OF WHO I WANT TO BE.

EVERY STRUGGLE, EVERY TRIAL, EVERY DAY
THAT SEEMS LIKE IT WILL NEVER END
IS PRODUCING SOMETHING BEAUTIFUL IN YOU.

"GOD WANTS TO DO SOMETHING BEAUTIFUL WITH YOUR PAIN.

WHAT PASSIONS HAS GOD PUT IN YOU?
WHAT MAKES YOU SMILE? WHAT MAKES YOU FEEL FREE?
THAT'S HOW YOU BUILD A LIFE OF LOVELY.

JESUS PAID FOR ME WITH HIS LIFE SO THAT

I WOULD BELONG TO NO ONE ELSE. . . .

HE HAS MADE MY LIFE WORTH LIVING.

IF YOU AREN'T EXPERIENCING PAIN, YOU AREN'T
EXPERIENCING BEAUTY. DARKNESS MAKES US
APPRECIATE THE BEAUTY OF THE LIGHT.

SOMETHING BEAUTIFUL HAPPENED WHEN I STARTED ASKING

JESUS TO BE MY FRIEND, MY CLOSE FRIEND.

_____

_____

_____

_____

_____

_____

_____

_____

_____

_____

_____

_____

_____

_____

_____

_____

_____

_____

_____

_____

_____

➤———————▶

CONFESSING TO GOD WHEN IT SEEMS HARD OR SCARY OR PAINFUL,
CONFESSING WHAT YOU WANT TO DO BUT WHAT FEELS TOO
CHALLENGING—IT'S WHAT HELPS YOU KEEP BUILDING.

GOD ASKED ME TO TRUST HIM. TO LET HIM
HOLD THE THINGS MY HANDS CANNOT GRASP.

I FEEL GOD PUSHING ME A BIT TO EMBRACE
MY BROKEN PLACES AND APPRECIATE MY WEAKNESSES
AS MUCH AS I APPRECIATE MY STRENGTHS.

WE ARE CREATED IN GOD'S IMAGE,
WONDERFULLY MADE ACCORDING TO HIS PLAN,
AND HE HAS NEVER MADE A MISTAKE.

WE RUN. WE STUMBLE AND FALL.
GOD PICKS US UP AGAIN AND AGAIN.

JESUS GIVES YOU STRENGTH TO ENDURE TODAY
AS YOU LOOK WITH HOPE TO THE FUTURE.

I KNOW NO GREATER JOY THAN LIVING LIFE WITH JESUS,
AND I LACK ABSOLUTELY NOTHING BECAUSE I HAVE HIM.

I WANT, MORE THAN ANYTHING ELSE, TO LOCK EYES WITH THIS
GOD WHO HAS TAKEN MY MOURNING AND TURNED IT INTO JOY.

YOU ARE ALWAYS LOVED, YOU ARE NEVER ALONE,

YOU ARE ENOUGH.

HE IS A GOD WHO PUTS EVERYTHING IN ITS RIGHT PLACE.

THE LONGER I LOOKED FOR LOVELY,
THE MORE I KEPT GOING, THE LESS I QUIT.
BUT I HAD TO KEEP CHOOSING TO PERSEVERE.